Phil Dampier has been writing about the royal family for 20 years. Between 1986 and 1991 he covered the royal beat for *The Sun*. He established a reputation for breaking major exclusive stories, and is renowned for his far-reaching contacts. As a freelance journalist for the last 15 years, he has travelled to more than 40 countries, following members of the House of Windsor, and his articles have been published in dozens of newspapers and magazines worldwide. He is currently royal editor of *New Idea*, one of Australia's biggest selling magazines. He lives in Kent with his partner Ann.

Ashley Walton was the royal correspondent of the *Daily Express* from 1979 to 1992. He travelled to every continent covering numerous tours, including the Queen and Prince Philip in India, Africa and China. He was one of the first reporters to identify a young Lady Diana Spencer as a future royal bride, and covered her last tour with Prince Charles to Korea in 1992. He was also among the first to reveal the romance between Prince Andrew and Sarah Ferguson. He lives in Hertfordshire with his wife Joan and their two sons.

DUKE OF HAZARD
THE WIT AND WISDOM OF
PRINCE PHILIP

Phil Dampier and
Ashley Walton

Book Guild Publishing
Sussex, England

First published in Great Britain in 2006 by
The Book Guild Ltd
Pavilion View
19 New Road
Brighton BN1 1UF

Second printing 2006
Third printing 2006
Fourth printing 2006
Fifth printing 2006
Sixth printing 2006
Seventh printing 2006
Eighth printing 2007
Ninth printing 2008
Tenth printing 2008
Eleventh printing 2009
Twelfth printing 2009
Thirteenth printing 2010
Fourteenth printing 2010

Typesetting in Garamond by
Keyboard Services, Luton, Bedfordshire

Printed in Great Britain by
CPI Antony Rowe

A catalogue record for this book is available from
The British Library

ISBN 978-1-84624-069-0

Contents

Sources and Acknowledgements

Some of these 'gaffes' were witnessed by the authors. Most have come from hours of combing through newspaper reports.

We are also grateful to material from the following books:

Butler, Peter, *The Wit of Prince Philip.* Leslie Frewin, London, 1965.

HRH Duke of Edinburgh, *Men, Machines and Sacred Cows.* Hamish Hamilton, London, 1984.

Prince Philip Speaks: Selected speeches 1956–59. Collins, London.

Brandreth, Gyles, *Philip and Elizabeth – Portrait of a marriage.* Century, London, 2004.

The Duke of Diplomacy

'If you stay here much longer, you will go home with slitty eyes.'

GAFFES ACROSS THE GLOBE

Prince Philip has been 'shocking all over the world' for years with his sledgehammer wit. There is no doubt that in today's politically correct society, many of his remarks could be regarded as racist. But we do not believe he means to cause offence.

His attitude, more likely, stems from a different age, when 'victims' of jokes were less sensitive, and those facing the horror of a world war had more important things to worry about.

The bottom line is that he doesn't care what people think about him; he is going to say what he wants anyway and to hell with the consequences. We find that refreshing in an era of dishonest politicians and manipulative spin-doctors.

As probably the world's most travelled man, he has certainly had a lot of material to work with.

So sit back and savour these classic insults across the globe.

During the Kenyan independence ceremonies in 1963 he was handing the African country over to Jomo Kenyatta. Just before midnight, when the chimes would signal independence and the Union Jack was due to be hauled down, Philip turned to the new leader and asked: 'Are you sure you want to go through with this?'

Questioned back in Britain by teenagers on a BBC show, Philip revealed: 'Kenyatta grinned all over his face and said, "No!"'

1963

To a Chilean representative who turned up to a Palace reception in an ordinary lounge suit for a black tie event: 'Why are you dressed like that?'

The confused guest replied: 'We are poor, I could not afford a dinner suit so my party told me to wear a lounge suit.'

Philip retorted: 'I suppose if they'd told you to wear a bathing suit, you would have done that too!'

Receiving the Freedom of Glasgow, he said: 'The freedom of the city is looked upon by those who give it and those who receive it as a very great honour indeed and the ceremony is full of charm and dignity.

'Unlike the ownership of Glasgow, which, I understand, can be obtained for a couple of drinks on a Saturday night.'

1955

The president of a Brazilian bowling club made a short speech in Portuguese after a banquet. Realising the Duke had not understood it, he presented him with an emblem and, summoning up his knowledge of English, explained: 'Balls, you know.'

Philip smiled and replied: 'And balls to you, sir!'

Proposing a toast at a dinner to celebrate the 300th anniversary of the resettlement of Jews in Britain: 'Here's the snag. Do I congratulate the ancestors of this community on having had the good sense to come here in the first place? Or do I congratulate the community on having stuck it here for three hundred years?'

1956

The Prince kept Pakistan's President Ayub Khan waiting several minutes on the Tarmac at Chakala Airport before he finally emerged from the plane, grinning and full of apologies: 'Sorry to keep you waiting. I usually change my trousers in the plane, otherwise I get out looking like a bag.'

1965

In Australia Philip was asked what he had done at two previous conferences for future industrial and community leaders – at Oxford in 1956 and Montreal in 1962. He replied: 'I flitted about, went to all the drinking parties, and rang a little bell sometimes.'

Asked whether businessmen visiting South America should wear a bowler hat or a sombrero, he said: 'It doesn't really matter. But it would be better to send a bowler-hatted man speaking Spanish than a man wearing a sombrero who could only speak English.'

April 1962

During a visit to Uruguay, Philip commented: 'I am convinced that the greatest contribution Britain has made to the national life of Uruguay was teaching the people football.'

1962

During a visit to Moscow to see President Yeltsin, security was so tight that no locals were allowed near Red Square. Eventually tourists were bussed in to swell the crowds. Philip asked someone in the crowd: 'Where are you from?'

When he replied 'Birmingham, if you can believe that', the Prince said: 'Yes I can – there are two blokes down there from Manchester!'

October 1994

Questioned on a BBC programme for teenagers in the 1960s he was asked if there was anywhere left in the world he'd like to visit.

He replied: 'Yes, I'd like to go to China, to Russia, and I haven't been to Japan.'

Q: 'How do you think you'd be received in places like this?'

Philip: 'Oh I think they'd be reasonably polite.'

Q: 'Do you think they would line the streets for instance?'

Philip: 'I wouldn't say that was essential.'

Introduced to French chef Regis Crepy in Ipswich, after he had laid on a superb spread of bacon, eggs, smoked salmon, kedgeree, croissants and pain au chocolat for invited guests, Philip told him: 'The French don't know how to cook breakfast.'

July 2002

At a Commonwealth conference, on meeting leaders of Nauru, a tiny South Pacific island dominated by a huge phosphate mine: 'So you're from Nauru, eh? Haven't they dug it all up yet?'

December 2003

To museum curator William Tennent on the Cayman Islands: 'Aren't most of you descended from pirates?'

December 1994

To Scottish driving instructor Robert Drummond in Oban: 'How do you keep the natives off the booze long enough to get them past the test?'

August 1995

In Nigeria he was asked by a reporter: 'So what do you think of Africa?'

He replied: 'I will pass on that if you don't mind.'

December 2003

On a tour of Budapest in Hungary he told a British tourist: 'You can't have been here that long – you haven't got a pot belly.'

1993

When Philip was asked if he would go to Moscow to help thaw the cold war, he replied: 'I would like to go to Russia very much – although the bastards murdered half my family.'

December 1967

During a speech in Hanover, he welcomed German Chancellor Helmut Kohl as '*Reichskanzler*' – Hitler's Nazi title.

April 1997

At a Buckingham Palace reception he asked cultural worker Sukhvinder Stubbs: 'And are you from Guyana?'

'Er, no I'm from India.'

Philip replied: 'I'm sure there are Indians in Guyana, they get everywhere don't they?'

June 2001

Visiting a food-canning factory in Gozo, Malta's sister island, staff presented him with two tins of spicy fruit and told him they would do the same thing every year for the rest of his life.

With a wry smile Philip retorted: 'You won't have to do that for very long then.'

November 2005

On a tour of the Racal-MESL electronics factory in Edinburgh he was shown a fuse box and said: 'It looks as though it was put in by an Indian.'

A week later at a charity lunch he said: 'What a load of fuss and nonsense. I meant to say cowboys. I just got my cowboys and Indians mixed up.'

August 1999

On a visit to Chippenham, Wiltshire, old soldier Jack Spencer told him: 'I used to serve in the Third Monmouthshire Regiment.'

Philip replied: 'What do you want to go to Wales for?'

December 2001

Touring a tomato-canning factory in Gozo he watched bottles of ketchup being labelled and packed. Spotting a worker wearing large white gumboots, he asked: 'What have you been doing – treading tomatoes?'

November 2005

In Berlin he was introduced to British youngsters studying climate change. He asked 16-year-old student Stuart Marks where he came from and he replied: 'Ballyclare in Northern Ireland.'

When 18-year-old Jack Logue gave the same answer, Philip quipped: 'At last! We've got two Irishmen in the same room who agree on something.'

What made his joke even more amusing was that earlier in the day the Queen had made a speech saying that 'simplistic stereotypes' should be avoided!

November 2004

To the smiling black man at a Commonwealth Day party: 'And what exotic part of the world do you come from?'

Former Tory candidate Lord Taylor of Warwick: 'I'm from Birmingham.'

March 1999

Perhaps Philip's most famous gaffe came in 1986 during a visit to China when he managed to insult a billion people and make headlines around the world.

He told 21-year-old British student Simon Kirby: 'If you stay here much longer, you will go home with slitty eyes.'

He also described Peking, which had just entertained him in grand style, as 'ghastly'.

1986

A month later, back in Britain, he told a World Wildlife Fund function: 'If it has got four legs and it's not a chair, if it has got two wings and it flies but it's not an aeroplane, and if it swims and it's not a submarine the Cantonese will eat it.'

1986

At a naval college at Malta for cadets he told them reassuringly: 'Rest assured – if you're no good they'll throw you out!'

November 2005

In Thailand to accept a conservation award, he told his hosts: 'Your country is one of the most notorious centres of trading in endangered species.'

1991

On a tour to Papua New Guinea, talking to a student who had trekked through the wildest mountain regions, he hinted at the natives' cannibalistic past, saying: 'You managed not to get eaten then?'

1998

On a visit to Canada he said: 'We don't come here for our health. We can think of other ways of enjoying ourselves.'

1976

On another tour of Canada he said of French Canadians: 'I can't understand a word they say. They slur all their words.'

1985

In Kenya, when offered a gift by a native woman, he looked at her quizzically and said: 'You ARE a woman aren't you?'

1984

On a visit down under, when asked if he would like to stroke a koala, Australia's national symbol, he said: 'No, I might get some ghastly disease.'

1992

In New Zealand he was invited to try his hand at sheep shearing. He declined, saying: 'Not on your life. I might nick him, and we've had quite enough mutton on the tour already thank you.'

Sikh royal policeman Sarinder Singh was at a Christmas party held by the Queen when Philip pointed at his turban and said: 'How on earth do you get that under your helmet?'

December 2003

In the Solomon Islands in the Pacific, when told the annual population growth was five per cent, he said: 'They must be out of their minds.'

1982

In India he visited Amritsar where 379 people were slaughtered by the British army in 1919. Shown a plaque, which read: 'This place is saturated with the blood of about 2,000 Hindu, Sikh and Moslem patriots who were martyred in a non-violent struggle to free India of British domination', Philip said: 'That's not right – the number is less.'

October 1997

On a South American tour in 1962 he was asked by a reporter if his visit to Argentina had been too brief.

He said: 'I have sixty days for this tour and I have visited ten countries. That makes six days in each country, and when you start blocking up traffic – well, the first day people enjoy it, but by the third they get bloody tired of it. The art of being a good guest is knowing when to leave.'

1962

In Canberra, Australia, Aborigine Bob Slockee played the didgeridoo and told Philip: 'I learned to play on a vacuum cleaner pipe.' To which the Duke replied: 'I hope it wasn't switched on.'

March 2000

Aussie farmer Steve Filelti demonstrated the use of a water gauge called a piezometer, only for Philip to crease up, declaring: 'A pissometer!'

March 2000

At a nearby fruit farm in Bourke, 500 miles from Sydney, he saw fruit packaged at a farm and quipped: 'Oh you're going in for this business of keeping people out of the food. No way you can open the bloody thing!'

March 2000

The Duke rejected a carving on a wooden chair made for him to commemorate the Queen's Golden Jubilee because it was decorated with olives, saying it was 'too foreign'.

March 2004

To a Sri Lankan priest at the North London Murugan Temple during the Queen's Golden Jubilee celebrations: 'Are you the Tamil Tigers?'

June 2002

Probably his best gaffe in recent years came on the 2002 tour of Australia with the Queen. At the Aboriginal Cultural Park in Cairns, Queensland, Philip asked Aboriginal leader William Brin: 'Do you still throw spears at each other?'

Phil Dampier was the only reporter who witnessed this classic and says: 'I'll never forget the look on William's face – it just fell and I knew the Prince had done it again. William just looked totally shocked.

'Philip was in great form and then strolled on to a fire dance ceremony with the Queen. As one performer rubbed sticks close to another's head, he joked: "You've set fire to him – this is just like being back in the Scouts."

'To be honest, at that point I was laughing so much I had to turn away. When I regained my composure I filed to the *Evening Standard* who splashed the story under the headline "Oh Philip" and the story was followed up all over the world. What made it even more memorable was that the next day the press pack met the Queen and Philip at a reception in Brisbane. As we stood in a huddle Philip wandered over, having heard about the coverage in that day's papers and came straight to the point.

' "The trouble with you lot is that you've got a total absence of humour, a complete lack of humour."

'When a photographer tried to placate him by

saying: "We all find your comments funny, sir," he barked back: "You just pretend to be funny!"

'He is a press officer's nightmare, but I'm so glad he is not afraid to speak his mind.'

February 2002

Occasionally Philip is on the receiving end... At a Buckingham Palace reception for World Cup cricketers, Philip came across a white player standing behind the West Indian team.

'Aren't you in the wrong team?' he asked.

'No, I play for Zimbabwe but I'm hung like a West Indian!'

The Duke roared with laughter.

June 1999

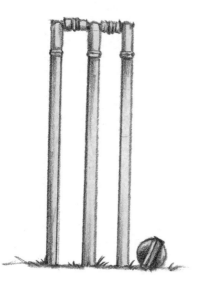

The Royal Salesman

'An expert in dontopedalogy.'

SELLING BRITAIN ABROAD AND AT HOME

Philip has described himself as an expert in 'dontopedalogy' – the art of 'opening your mouth and putting your foot in it'.

In many ways his honesty has been his greatest asset. But his inability to keep his thoughts to himself has also landed him in trouble, especially when he is supposed to be promoting, not knocking Great Britain plc.

As the Queen opened the new £18 million British Embassy in Berlin, Philip told guests at a reception: 'It's a vast waste of space.'

July 2000

On an official visit to Texas to support British industry he declared: 'I'm not here to flog anything.'

Asked on the same trip about the state of Britain, he said: 'We are down on our uppers!'

March 1966

Left wing MP Tom Littlewood called the Duke a 'useless reactionary parasite' as a result of the following remark: 'I'm sick of making excuses for this country.'

1966

In the early 1960s, as Britain suffered a time of economic gloom, Philip caused a national scandal by urging the nation to work harder, telling a group of industrialists: 'Just at this moment we are suffering a national defeat comparable to any lost military campaign, and, what is more, self-inflicted. Gentlemen, I think it is about time we pulled our fingers out.'

October 1961

After opening a new City and Guilds of London Institute he told the foreman: 'Get weaving, I've done my bit!'

At a lunch held by the National Union of Manufacturers: 'We are certainly not a nation of nitwits. In fact wits are our greatest single asset.

He once told the Ancient Society of Merchant Venturers: 'The "stop everything" brigade is as strong as ever, it is up to you to prove that the "start something" society is undismayed.'

After succeeding Sir Harold Hartley as president of the Institute of Chemical Engineers, Philip said: 'Now the advancement of science has gone from the sublime to the gorblimey!'

At the AGM of the Automobile Association, of which he was president, he said: 'I've been made to sit in this room next door all the morning, listening to the most enormous amount of bunkum … except for the chairman of course … and at last it's my turn to add my quota to the bunkum.'

1958

If anyone has a new idea in this country, there are twice as many people who advocate putting a man with a red flag in front of it.'

1960

Opening the Design Centre for British Industries, the Prince remarked: 'It's no good shutting your eyes and saying: "Britain is best" three times a day after meals, and expecting it to be so.'

1956

To a group of businessmen: 'Many look upon research as something which might help a conjurer to produce an elephant instead of a rabbit out of his hat.

'It does sometimes, but most of the time it is helping the conjurer produce a bigger and better rabbit out of a smaller and cheaper hat.'

February 1956

Philip told one group of industrialists: 'America invented the term "yes men" while Britain is full of "no men".'

In the same year he asked National Coal Board bosses: 'How much longer are you going to exploit every feature of this land purely for gain?'

1956

'The trouble with senior management to an outsider is that there are too many one-ulcer men holding down two-ulcer jobs!'

May 1963

'Sacred cows are all right in certain paddocks. But they should not be welcome in the field of industry and commerce.'

1963

Visiting a Welsh steelworks he pressed the button to start a new blast furnace turbo-blower. He then signed the work sheet: 'Philip – turbine driver – 6 to 2 shift.'

1962

To the Modular Society luncheon: 'It seems I have a terrible reputation for telling people what they ought to be doing.'

1962

Opening a wind tunnel for aircraft research he told technicians: 'We want "yes" men as well as "no" men, and we want people who can see further than the end of their noses and further than the end of a Ministry of Supply vote.'

1955

On his 39th birthday, speaking at the New York Waldorf-Astoria hotel after opening the British Exhibition: 'Whatever tourists and tourist guides may tell you, Britain is not just an old country of tottering ruins inhabited by idle roués in eye glasses.

'Nor is it a country where yokels quaff ale by the tankard outside rickety pubs, where all soldiers are dressed in scarlet tunics and spend their time marching up and down for the benefit of visitors from abroad.

'Scotland is not entirely peopled by huge red-headed men in kilts with hairy legs, who drink whisky when they are not playing the bagpipes or tossing the caber.

'There are certainly several harps in Wales and many fine singers too. But the eisteddfods are only a relaxation!'

June 1960

Philip has no time for wafflers. In 1956 he launched the Duke of Edinburgh Conference on the 'Social Responsibilities of Industry', and after one boss had made a badly prepared three-minute speech, Philip said: 'I'm afraid I didn't quite get the sense of that, would you mind repeating it?'

1956

Head of the Family

'A cantankerous old sod.'

ON HIMSELF AND OTHER ROYALS

Philip is a firm believer in 'toughening up' children and teenagers to prepare them for the rigours of the real world. His Duke of Edinburgh's Award scheme challenges them to push themselves to their limits. He sent his own children to the harsh Scottish school of Gordonstoun, which he loved as a pupil, to foster their physical, as well as mental, qualities.

No surprise then that his own family, and indeed he himself, can also be targets of his verbal onslaughts.

In 2001, on a visit to Cardiff to promote the Duke of Edinburgh's Awards, he admitted he was a 'cantankerous old sod'.

Asked if the scheme might attract more participants if it were not named after him, he replied: 'Whatever you call it, some people will think it is rubbish while some people would not be worried about this connection with this cantankerous old sod up here!'

February 2001

As the Queen kept chatting to a local dignitary in Belize, Central America, while Philip waited to board the *Royal Yacht Britannia*, he lost his patience and snapped at her: 'Get a move on!'

February 1944

After a tour of Australia and New Zealand: 'As so often happens, I discover that it would have been better to keep my mouth shut.'

1968

The day before his wedding in November 1947 the Prince was stopped for speeding on Constitution Hill just beside Buckingham Palace. Contritely, and truthfully, he told the officer: 'Sorry, but I've got an appointment with the Archbishop of Canterbury!'

November 1947

During a dinner for the Welsh Guards, which was also attended by the Queen, he asked: 'What is unique about this regiment?'

Then he answered the question himself: 'It is the only one in which the Colonel is legally married to the Colonel-in-Chief.'

1965

Royal biographer Gyles Brandreth told how Philip introduced him to the Queen. ' "This is Gyles Brandreth," said the Duke.

'As Her Majesty proffered me a tightly gloved hand, and with a slightly nervous smile, murmured an almost inaudible "How do you do?" her consort continued: "Apparently he's writing about you."

'The Duke paused and leant forward towards his wife's ear: "Be warned, he's going to cut you into pieces." '

2002

Speaking about his school days: 'I was not the least aware I was any different from any of the others. It's true I had this title of Prince, but it's surprising how you can live it down. My favourite subject at school was avoiding unnecessary work.'

1965

Asked at a Foreign Press Association lunch whether he thought the royal family showed sufficient interest in the arts: 'There is no art form in this country that has not got some member of the royal family at the head of it.

'Mind you, not every member of the royal family goes in for each art, but they do tend to divide it up ... we live in what virtually amounts to a museum.'

1964

Addressing the London City Livery Club: 'Just before coming out to lunch today I was asked by my wife where I was going. I said I was going to the City Livery Club; so she said, "Oh! Am I a Liveryman?"

'And I replied: "No, I'm sorry you are not, you are only a livery woman."'

1948

On a visit to Scotland Yard he was asked if he would have his fingerprints taken and put on the souvenir file. He agreed, saying: 'Let's choose an interesting finger!'

A senior policeman said that they had already got Princess Margaret's fingerprints.

'Good for you!' said Philip.

1960

At a press reception in Canberra, Australia: 'I suppose I'd better watch my saltier adjectives – am I being interviewed?'

1963

Opening the Man-Made Fibres Building Exhibition in Leeds he pointed to his own balding head saying: 'I'm not a very good man-made fibres man myself!'

When Philip, on a clay pigeon shoot at Sand-ringham, was asked about bruises on his face, by a journalist, he barked: 'Do I look bloody ill?'

April 2004

'I didn't particularly want to go into the army – I didn't fancy walking much.'

1965

Shown a portrait of himself by artist Stuart Pearson Wright, he exclaimed: 'Gadzooks!'

Asked if he'd caught his likeness he replied: 'I bloody well hope not!'

On another occasion he asked the artist: 'Why have you given me a great schonk?'

July 2003

To a group of industrialists: 'I have never been noticeably reticent about talking on subjects about which I know nothing.'

October 1961

'People think there's a rigid class system here, but dukes have even been known to marry chorus girls. Some have even married Americans.'

December 2000

Philip once managed to forget Charles's birthday –
shortly before joining him for lunch on the day.
Signing the visitors' book at a homeless centre in
London he asked: 'What's the date today – is it
the thirteenth?'

'No, it's the fourteenth,' said the Queen adding,
'Charles's birthday, remember?'

'Oh yes, of course,' said Philip – before setting
off to mark Charles's forty-ninth birthday aboard
the *Royal Yacht Britannia.*

November 1997

On being told that Prince Edward had secured a
place at Jesus College, Cambridge with only a grade
C and two Ds at A-level, he quipped: 'What a
friend we have in Jesus.'

1983

When 'comic' Aaron Barschak gatecrashed Prince
William's 21st birthday party at Windsor Castle,
Edward was the only senior royal not there. It was
noted that if Barschak had been a suicide bomber
and had killed everyone present, Edward would
have become king. Philip told guests his son must
have been behind the stunt.

He joked: 'It's bound to have been Edward. Only
the boy could have coached such a rotten
performance out of someone.'

June 2003

On the Queen's Christmas speeches: 'Short of hiring a line of chorus girls and calling it *The Queen Show*, what more can you do?'

On Fergie, shortly before her marriage to Andrew the Prince remarked: 'I think she'll be a great asset. For one thing, she is capable of becoming self-employed.'

1986

On seeing plans for the interior of Andy and Fergie's house at Sunninghill Park: 'It looks like a tart's bedroom.'

1988

'Her [Duchess of York's] behaviour was a bit odd. I don't see her because I don't see much point.'

May 1999

At a drinks party in Windsor Castle he was offered cocktail sausages by a red-haired waitress. 'Good god, I can't take canapés from you – you're Fergie,' he roared.

July 2001

At the Guildhall luncheon to celebrate their 50th wedding anniversary he said: 'You can take it from me that the Queen has the quality of tolerance in abundance.'

1997

In New York in 1960 he explained he had to get home to celebrate the Queen's official birthday.

'Don't ask me to explain why it is that she has an official birthday in June, when her proper birthday is in April. You'll just have to accept it like cricket, pounds, shillings and pence, and other quaint, but practical British customs.'

1960

In Australia he met a couple introduced as Mr and Dr Robinson, and the husband explained: 'My wife is a doctor of philosophy and much more important than I am.'

Philip replied: 'Ah yes, we have that trouble in our family too!'

1954

'Prince Charles is a romantic, I'm a pragmatist. That means we do see things differently.'

May 1999

When asked on a Canadian tour if he knew the Scilly Isles off the coast of Cornwall, he replied: 'My son ... er ... owns them.'

On a tour of Bolivia he was asked why he had not brought Princess Margaret's husband, professional photographer Lord Snowdon, as his official snapper.

'He has another job ... Britain is a democracy,' he said. 'I get the photographer I'm given.'

Later, in Chile, he appealed to a local photographer to stop following him so closely saying: 'We have one in the family already.'

Of Princess Anne: 'If it doesn't fart or eat hay she's not interested.'

'Gadzooks! Why have you given me a great schonk?'

The Headmaster

'Over the years Philip has not been afraid to dish out a caning
to teachers and pupils alike.'

EDUCATION

Over the years Philip has not been afraid to dish out a caning to teachers and pupils alike. Unlike Tony Blair he does not believe in 'education, education, education' just for the sake of it.

He once said: 'The conception of a university as simply a means to enhance the prosperity of the state reduces higher education to the level of cattle breeding.'

Although he became head boy at Gordonstoun, Philip has only honorary degrees and believes in the importance of spiritual and physical well-being as much as academic achievements.

After opening a £500,000 extension to the Heriot-Watt College in Edinburgh, the Prince got stuck in a lift between two floors. He commented: 'This could only happen in a technical college.'

July 1958

Addressing pupils of a school in Ipswich, he urged them to keep an open, unbigoted, inquiring mind, admit mistakes and be reasonably modest about success. Then he added: 'It is traditional on these occasions for me to give you a bit of advice, which you will equally traditionally ignore.'

May 1956

Opening the Chesterfield College of Technology he said: 'A lot of time and energy has been spent on arranging for you to listen to me take a long time to declare open a building, which everybody knows is open already. Tomorrow, to all intents and purposes, everything will be back to normal.

'That rather makes it look as if we are all wasting our time and yet we can all give perfectly good reasons why this ceremony was arranged and I'm sure you've all got perfectly good reasons for being here.'

November 1958

At London University the Prince sat through almost three hours of films about technology, the principles of ultra-sonics and later said: 'I was most interested to learn that the X-ray goes in one ear and out of the other.'

At the opening of a National Playing Fields Association exhibition: 'You planners and designers may believe that you've designed the perfect layout for the perfect playing field as seen through adult eyes. But I can assure you that it may prove deadly dull to a child of four.'

1954

On the opening of yet another playing field, in Devon: 'There is no need to have a Rolls-Royce scheme. You want a reasonably flat piece of ground with sufficient grass on it and some posts, and if you get these, you're half way home. Put on the fancy waistcoats later.'

On being installed as chancellor of Edinburgh University: 'In education, if in nothing else, the Scotsman knows what is best for him. Indeed, only a Scotsman can really survive a Scottish education.'

November 1953

Accepting an honorary degree as Doctor of Science at Reading University: 'It must be pretty well known that I never earned an honest degree in my life and I certainly never made any effort to gain an honorary one.'

To the boys of exclusive private Uppingham School in Rutland: 'Everybody has got to understand a little bit about science or he can't understand what the hell goes on around him.

'Unless you know something about science you won't get into the House of Commons.'

1957

'University education is merely so much vocational training unless it puts some fire into your belly.'

November 1961

In Edinburgh to a 1953 meeting of the Library Association: 'In 1951 I was a very bad president of the Library Association; I was very bad because I spent most of that year at sea and as far as the Library Association is concerned, in more ways than one.'

1953

In 1947 Philip took Princess Elizabeth to his old school Cheam where he introduced his old head, Rev H.M.S. Taylor and said to her: 'The man used to cane me!'

The Rev replied: 'I had to cane him more than once – he got into all the usual scrapes.'

1947

At the Fir Vale Comprehensive School in Sheffield, which at one time had an appalling academic record, he asked a group of parents: 'Were you here in the bad old days?'

When two women nodded he boomed: 'That's why you can't read and write then!'

May 2003

At the University of York he told bemused onlookers: 'It is surprising the way things have changed since I first became chancellor of the university fifty years ago.' The only problem was he was not chancellor and it was the 40th anniversary.

February 2003

At the opening of a Jewish school in Hertfordshire: 'Holidays are curious things aren't they? You send children to school to get them out of your hair. Then they come back for holidays and make life difficult for parents. That is why holidays are set so they are just about the limit of your endurance.'

July 2000

On a visit to University of Sussex in Brighton he confessed he was driven potty by TV controls, saying: 'The only thing you need to know is how to turn it on and they try to hide it from you.'

March 2001

The Duke was touring Linacre Primary School in Bootle, Merseyside, when he asked a caretaker: 'Can you manage to control all these vandals?'

July 1998

Chatting to pupils from Queen Anne's School in Reading, Berkshire, who wear blood-red uniforms: 'It makes you all look like Dracula's daughters!'

October 1998

Unveiling a plaque at the University of Hertford-shire's new Hatfield campus he declared: 'During the blitz a lot of shops had their windows blown in and sometimes they put up notices saying, "More open than usual".

'I now declare this place more open than usual.'

November 2003

'This could only happen in a technical college.'

The Gaffer

'I served in the Royal Navy during the war.'

INSULTS AND POLITICALLY INCORRECT
OBSERVATIONS

No one is safe when 'The Gaffer' gets going.

Wheelchair users, old soldiers, young children and people caught up in tragic disasters have all been victims of his caustic, sometimes cruel comments.

He thinks he is being funny and is often amazed by the reaction to his remarks. But many on the receiving end have been left bewildered, and some even in tears by the viciousness of the royal tongue.

Swedish tourist Ronnie Cahana waved to Philip as he was driving his horse-drawn carriage back to the stables at Windsor Castle and proudly shouted: 'Good morning, sir, my little girl is six today!'

The Duke replied: 'So what?' and drove off, leaving little Kitra Cahana in tears.

February 1996

While he was painting a portrait of the Prince, artist John Orr was told by him that cannibals in the days of Empire got mad cow disease but 'it just disappeared when they stopped eating each other'.

September 1996

At a Buckingham Palace reception he met smoke alarm campaigner Sue Parkin, who lost her two sons in a fire.

Philip told her: 'They're a damn nuisance – I've got one in my bathroom and every time I run my bath the steam sets it off and I've got the fire brigade at the door.'

June 1998

When he became a Fellow of the Royal College of Surgeons, the president presented him with a silver replica of an old-fashioned bleeding cup, saying: 'May it please Your Royal Highness to accept this bleeding cup.'

Philip replied: 'Well I can only say, it's bloody kind of you!'

Visiting a Manchester textiles group, the Prince greeted the chairman of the knitting division: 'So you're the head knit!'

July 1965

At a Buckingham Palace reception to mark 50 years of his Duke of Edinburgh's Award scheme, he was asked if it was still relevant. He replied: 'The point is young people are the same as they always were. They are just as ignorant.'

October 2005

He once described a party at Lambeth Palace, home of the Archbishop of Canterbury, as 'a surplice of bishops'.

At a reception he asked an old soldier proudly wearing his many medals: 'Have you got any on the back too?'

In Australia, on a visit to some caves, he was warned to beware of the drips.

'Oh those! I've run into plenty in my life,' he quipped.

Commenting on the view from Buckingham Palace after a large building had replaced what used to be a brewery: 'I am not quite sure which is worse, the sight of what is there now, or the smell which used to be there.'

During the recession in the early 1980s he proclaimed: 'A few years ago everybody was saying we must have more leisure, everybody's working too much.

'Now that everybody's got more leisure time they are complaining they are unemployed. People don't seem to make up their minds what they want.'

1981

After meeting students in Brunei about to study in Britain: 'I don't know how they are going to integrate in places like Glasgow and Sheffield.'

September 1998

At a Buckingham Palace garden party he was introduced to a perfectly respectable building boss who told him he was retiring after years in a business renowned for cowboy operators.

'Do you have any friends left?' asked Philip.

July 2003

At a breakfast to mark the 200th anniversary of St James's barbers, Truefit & Hill: 'There's an interesting bunch of you who no doubt come here to have your hair cut. Although there are a couple of obvious exceptions ... you people from Iceland no doubt come here to have your beards trimmed.'

October 2005

On a tour of the newly-built *Queen Mary II* he was shown the cruise liner's hospital and was told that around four people die each year on Cunard's ships, often terminally ill passengers.

Gazing into the mortuary fridge he joked: 'So they book one of these in advance, eh?'

Later, after being told there were 21 bars on board, he told purser Claudette Kirkwood: 'You could have one big pub crawl.'

January 2004

On a visit to the Adelphi theatre in London he met the scantily clad dancing girls of the hit show *Chicago*.

'Where on earth do you keep your microphones?' he asked.

As the laughs flowed he continued: 'If the show has been running two years why do you still need rehearsals?'

March 1999

On his way to a Sotheby's lunch in New York he encountered a man clutching a placard declaring: 'Sotheby's sold me a fake!'

Philip muttered: 'Only one?'

March 1996

When 65-year-old car park attendant Bob Proudfoot failed to recognise Philip at Cambridge University and asked for a pass, the Duke barked: 'You bloody silly fool.'

February 1997

The design of the original 50p piece was changed to 'pence' after Philip, then president of the Royal Mint Advisory Committee said: 'I don't like that little "p".'

December 1972

He caused uproar after attacking government plans to crack down on guns in the wake of the Dunblane massacre when 16 schoolchildren were shot dead. He said it was unfair on shooting club members who were no more dangerous than cricketers or squash players.

'If a cricketer, for instance, suddenly decided to go into a school and batter a lot of people to death with a cricket bat, which he could do very easily, I mean are you going to ban cricket bats?' he asked.

It was then revealed he clearly knew his remarks on BBC radio would cause offence as he told his interviewer off air: 'That will really set the cat among the pigeons won't it?'

December 1996

At a youth festival in Cardiff Castle he was introduced to a group of youngsters from the British Deaf Association who were standing near a noisy Caribbean steel band. He pointed to the musicians and commented: 'Deaf? If you are near there, no wonder you are deaf.'

His remark caused deep offence but he later explained to biographer Gyles Brandreth that his comment had been taken out of context and that his own mother was deaf.

May 1999

Interviewed in a TV documentary to mark the 50th anniversary of V-J Day he recalled how shipmates died or were wounded during action.

'It was part of the fortunes of war,' he said. 'We didn't have counsellors rushing around every time somebody let off a gun, asking, "Are you all right – are you sure you don't have a ghastly problem?" You just got on with it.'

His remarks were seen as a clear attack on modern-day stress counselling.

August 1995

'Will you turn that fucking horn off?' said to a chauffeur tooting his horn during a royal visit to Morocco.

October 1980

At Buckingham Palace, BBC newsreader Michael Buerk helped present Duke of Edinburgh's Gold Awards.

'Do you know anything about it?' Philip asked him.

When the respected broadcaster replied that he did, Philip barked: 'Well, that's more than you know about anything else then.'

2004

Philip appears to have developed an obsession about people in wheelchairs. He approached 82-year-old retired farmer James Banfield during a Buckingham Palace garden party and pointed to his wheelchair, saying: 'That's the best way to get around this place!'

Mr Banfield, wearing a top hat and tails for the event, said later: 'What a funny thing to say to me.'

July 2005

On a walkabout in Exeter during the Queen's 2002 Jubilee celebrations, Philip met blind Susan Edwards, 55, who was in a wheelchair with her 8-year-old guide dog Natalie by her side.

'Do you know they now do eating dogs for the anorexic?' Philip inquired.

May 2002

Meeting a group of nursing home residents in Bristol he asked wheelchair-bound Jackie Henderson: 'Do people trip over you?'

He then asked about her electric wheelchair, saying: 'Do you need a licence for that?'

March 2002

At a Buckingham Palace garden party he began talking to a middle-aged man in a wheelchair and asked: 'Why do you have a stick if you're in a wheelchair?'

July 2000

Sandie Hollands, a 29-year-old who suffers from a muscle-wasting disease, was at the wrong end of Philip's wit during a visit to the Royal Agricultural Show in South Wales.

'You are a bit of a menace in that thing,' he told her, looking at her wheelchair.

When she replied: 'I am a good driver,' Philip pointed to the metal foot-rests and said, 'They catch people's ankles.'

July 2004

Philip was on top form during a visit to the University of East London during the Golden Jubilee year. He asked if someone was a lecturer, and when told no, commented: 'That's right, he doesn't have enough hair.'

Shown pellets used in construction made out of recycled sewage, he joked: 'What do they eat in East London to get that?'

When he was shown a new environmentally friendly toilet using air instead of water to flush, he asked: 'Where does the wind come from?'

May 2002

At Salford University he met 13-year-old schoolboy Andrew Adams who said he would like to be an astronaut.

'You could do with losing a little bit of weight,' Philip told the chubby youngster.

July 2001

The Duke upset survivors on the ground of the Lockerbie disaster at a memorial ceremony when he told them: 'People usually say that after a fire it is the water damage that is worst. We are still drying out Windsor Castle.' (After the fire in 1992.)

June 1993

During a long boring speech at a dinner, Philip called over toastmaster Ivor Spencer and said: 'At least you get paid for this!'

February 1994

Meeting members of a Bangladeshi youth club in London, Philip sat among them and enquired: 'So, who's on drugs here?'

He then pointed at 14-year-old Shahin Ullah and smirked: 'HE looks as if he's on drugs.'

December 2002

At a party in aid of the World Wide Fund for Nature in Toronto, Canada, he chatted to pretty fashion writer Serena French and told her: 'I suppose you'll be looking out for people wearing mink coats then?'

When somebody remarked that no one would wear fur to such an event, Philip quipped: 'Well, you never know what they're wearing underneath.'

He then leaned towards Serena and asked: 'You're not wearing mink knickers are you?'

October 1993

Spotting a group of Labour women MPs at a Palace drinks party, who were wearing badges marked 'Ms' he said: 'Ah, so this is feminist corner then.'

July 2000

Teenager George Barlow wrote to the Queen inviting her to Romford, Essex, and became the toast of the town when she accepted. When Philip was introduced to the nervous 14-year-old during the visit he barked: 'Ah, you're the one who wrote the letter. So you can write then? Ha, ha. Well done.'

March 2003

On a visit to the Science Museum with the Queen to open a new wing he was shown some robots that kept bumping into each other.

'They're not mating are they?' he asked a professor.

June 2000

Opening a new £56 million maths centre at Cambridge University he quipped: 'This is a lot less expensive than the Dome. And I think it's going to be a great deal more useful.'

In an interview with *Country Life* magazine he told how he once tried abstract painting.

'It was very time consuming because I just sat there with a blank canvas wondering what to paint. And then I thought that whatever I do, some psychiatrist will come along and say: "My God, that chap should be in an institution!"'

May 1994

At a Buckingham Palace reception Philip told Euro MP Michael Cashman the European Union was 'all balls'.

Talking about fisheries policy he blasted: 'We should be like the Icelandic people and patrol our waters with gunboats.'

September 2004

To the Scottish WI: 'British women can't cook.'

1961

To skint student Alison Nisbet, 21 at Edinburgh University: 'Why don't you go and live in a hostel to save cash?'

February 1997

On a visit to the Smile internet bank offices in Manchester he said: 'Some banks might be like sweat shops but this one is very luxurious.'

October 2000

He told an audience of Scottish architects: 'I think it is worth remembering, when you look around, that everything that has not been made by God, has probably been perpetrated by an architect.'

1958

At a laundry exhibition: 'Which is the shrinking machine?'

'You have to wait until kingdom come if you wait for officialdom.'

1961

'Privilege is privilege, whether it is due to money or intellect or whether you have six toes.'

1963

'It is my invariable custom to say something flattering to begin with so that I shall be excused if by any chance I put my foot in it later on.'

1956

Laying the foundation stone of the Victory Ex-Services Club: 'I don't know that I'm very good at laying foundation stones. I only hope this one will be reasonably well laid when it's there, and that all the rest of the building will be better laid … now where do you want it?'

1954

Opening the Animal Health Trust's farm in Stock, Essex, he said: 'Ladies and gentlemen, it gives me the greatest pleasure to declare this laboratory open, and if someone will lend me a key I will unlock it.'

December 1957

As the Queen opened the new £43 million City Hall near Tower Bridge, London, assembly chairman Trevor Phillips said to the Duke: 'You should have a look at the view, it's wonderful.'

Philip replied: 'It's terrible, look at all those buildings.'

July 2002

While waiting for the arrival of Russian President Vladimir Putin in Horse Guards Parade, Philip told a joke involving a blind man and his dog ... to among others, blind Home Secretary David Blunkett.

Apparently he found it hilarious.

July 2003

At a Palace reception for MPs, Philip asked new-comer Parmjit Dhanda what he did before entering Parliament.

When he said he had been a student and trade union official Philip commented: 'You didn't do anything then.'

Mr Dhanda then asked Philip: 'What did you do before becoming Duke of Edinburgh?'

Philip replied: 'I served in the Royal Navy during the war,' and then, according to some eyewitnesses, gave the 31-year-old MP a two-fingered V-sign before walking off with a broad smile on his face!

November 2002

At a dinner party at Broadlands, home of Mount-batten heir Nicholas Knatchbull, Philip started ranting about Tony Blair, saying: 'He promises education, education, education, but never delivers. Bring back Mrs T, that's what I say. There's no one quite like Mrs T.'

Earlier, sitting down, he said: 'Bugger the table plan, give me my dinner!'

April 2004

'Fox-hunting is a curious thing to ban, because of all the blood sports, it's the only one where the people following it don't come anywhere near a wild animal at all.'

June 2004

He was held up for an hour when a train mowed down and killed 20 sheep. When he arrived at the Wildscreen Trust in Bristol to receive an award for his work preserving wildlife, he joked: 'This is a new excuse – there were sheep on the line.'

October 1996

When Philip was travelling with biographer Gyles Brandreth he spotted a man opening a car door for a woman.

The Duke said: 'If you see a man opening a car door for a woman, it means one of two things: It's either a new woman or a new car!'

October 2004

Tony Blair's spin-doctor Alastair Campbell was on a barge with the Duke and asked him: 'Do you reckon you could drive one of these?'

Philip snorted: 'I was a bloody naval commander!'

March 2004

'Ah, so this is feminist corner then.'

The Entertainer

'I wish he'd turn the microphone off.'

SHOWBIZ FRIENDS, SPORTING TALES AND TV TURN-OFFS

A famous black and white TV clip from a Variety Club lunch shows Philip creased up with laughter as Tommy Cooper goes through his routine.

In the company of showbiz stars and sporting friends he gives as good as he gets – and of course he loves pretty women!

To singer Tom Jones: 'Do you gargle with pebbles to sing that way?'

At a Variety Club lunch in honour of *Crazy Gang* star Bud Flanagan, who, with boxing promoter Jack Solomons, owned a string of betting shops, the Prince said: 'I don't know if anybody noticed but Bud Flanagan is looking better dressed and more prosperous than ever before. I gather this is from working on the other side of a betting shop counter!'

1964

To a golfing society dinner: 'Prepare for a shock ... I do not play golf.'

1949

Surrounded by glamorous females as he presented the British Academy Film Awards: 'This is the first time that this function has been organised by the new Society of Film and Television Arts, and so, as president, I thought it would be a good idea to come along and keep an eye on things.

'I haven't been disappointed either as I have already noticed several very nice things to keep my eye on!'

1960

At a reception in Lahore, Pakistan, he said: 'I am looking forward to attending the horse show, which is in progress here. I would have perhaps liked to take part in a game of polo but I am very unfit, and in any case, one tombstone in Lahore to a misguided prince who came a cropper is probably enough.'

1959

To the Cricket Club conference: 'The last time I played in a village match I was given out lbw first ball. That is the sort of umpiring that should be looked into.'

'The only active sport, which I follow, is polo – and most of the work's done by the pony!'

April 1965

'If you want to cook up a good international row, have a good sporting meeting.'

June 1962

At a dinner to celebrate the 25th anniversary of the British Empire and Commonwealth Games Federation, shortly before the 1958 Empire Games in Cardiff: 'To keep a balance in Wales between sport and culture they have organised a Festival of Wales at the same time, so that anyone who gets bored with hammer throwing can go and listen to the harp.'

1958

On his opening of the Melbourne Olympics in 1956: 'I made, if I may say so, the best speech of my life. It consisted of exactly twelve words!'

After a Royal Variety Performance he shook 45-year-old Donny Osmond's hand and said: 'Will someone please give some grey hair to this kid!'

December 2003

On a tour of Jersey with the Queen, Philip met John Nettles, who played the part of island detective Jim Bergerac in the BBC series. He told him: 'There are so many murders in your show I'm surprised there's anyone left in Jersey.'

On a visit to the set of *EastEnders* he asked actor Adam Woodyatt, who plays Ian Beale: 'Are you an actor or an operator?'

November 2001

For a TV special he told actress Joanna Lumley: 'There's a maddening thing called talent. Some people have it and some don't. Sometimes you have to sit there green with envy that you can't do things they can do.'

April 2000

Chatting to Windsor neighbour Elton John he was told the singer had got rid of an Aston Martin in Watford's gold colours: 'Oh, it's you that owns that ghastly car – we often see it when driving to Windsor Castle.'

June 2001

The Queen and Philip watched Elton John top the bill at the 73rd Royal Variety Performance and play three songs with his back to the royal box. 'I wish he'd turn the microphone to one side,' said the Queen.

'I wish he'd turn the microphone off!' said Philip.

November 2001

At the unveiling of a commemorative statue to the late comedian Eric Morecambe, the Duke spotted Sir Robin Day's name among those carved into the plinth.

'Is this where you're going to be buried?' he asked the bow-tied interrogator.

October 1999

Chatting to schoolchildren about *EastEnders*: 'Oh no, I never watch that.'

October 1998

On a visit to Nottingham Forest Football Club he was shown a statue of ex-manager Brian Clough and the bulging trophy room.

'I suppose I would get in a lot of trouble if I were to melt them down,' he quipped.

December 1999

As a young captain of Chelsea in the 1960s Terry Venables introduced Philip to his team before a match and remarked of a newcomer that he was 'playing his first game'.

Philip exclaimed: 'You mean he has never played football before?'

February 1964

When he was asked to put a sponsor's sticker on his boat during Cowes week he exploded: 'I am not coming back here if I have to put a sticker on my boat again!'

August 1985

Sometimes he is surprisingly PC. In an interview with Yeovil Town Football Club he said: 'I cannot see any conceivable reason why women should not play the game if they feel like it. I can see no reason why women should not make equally good referees and umpires.'

September 1998

On a visit to Arsenal's ground he saw Prodigy star Leeroy Thornhill wearing a shirt in a pro-celebrity game with the sponsor's name 'Dreamcast' on it.

'Is Dreamcast the name of the team?' he asked.

February 2000

The Original Green Man

'It makes a rather splendid picture to see members of the Institute of Fuel smoking like the proverbial chimneys.'

A deep thinker on the environment, in many ways Philip has been ahead of his time. Many of the ideas he suggested in the 1950s and 1960s are now fashionable in the 21st century.

His views on health matters, pollution, traffic, agriculture and architecture paved the way for his son Prince Charles to saddle up on his own hobby horse.

This visionary classic in 1956 to New Zealand school pupils foretold modern day fears about junk food and childhood obesity.

'In this modern age, no one has to use their arms or legs very much, except to lift their food into their mouths – or possibly to catch the bus.'

1956

Speaking to a group of British Airways staff at a Palace garden party he referred to the noise made by Concorde as it flew over Windsor Castle and said: 'I must be the only person in Britain glad to see the back of that plane.'

July 2004

At the opening of the new City Hall in London he talked to members of the London assembly about the capital's traffic problems and said: 'Of course the problem with London is the tourists. They cause the congestion. They block the streets. If we could just stop the tourism we could stop the congestion.'

July 2002

Speaking in New York about a London taxi he was about to buy, which ran on liquid gas, he was asked: 'Keeping up with the times?'

He replied: 'Absolutely not – keeping ahead of them!'

March 1998

Talking to the Bedford-based Aircraft Research Association he said: 'When you travel as much as I do you appreciate the improvements in aircraft design of less noise and more comfort – provided you don't travel in something called economy class, which sounds ghastly.'

May 2002

Opening a new check-in hall at an Irish airport he said: 'I don't know if you have spent the night in one of these airports but they make the seats in such a way you can't lie down. Sitting down's pretty uncomfortable as well.'

November 1998

At the University of Edinburgh he opened a training centre and proclaimed: 'All these jobs will bring in a lot of cars. You'll have to do something about the roads.'

August 2002

At the Royal Society of Arts he questioned the efficiency of wind farms, saying: 'But will they ever produce enough electricity to make the turbines go round?'

May 2001

Four years later, talking at the RSA about climate change he said: 'When they put up a whole farm of windmills off the north-east coast of Norfolk, which is on the main migratory route to Scandinavia, are we going to get sliced up ducks coming across?'

June 2005

At Windsor Castle during a discussion about GM foods he said: 'The introduction of the grey squirrel has done far more damage than a genetically modified piece of potato.'

June 2000

At the Palace of Holyroodhouse in Edinburgh he met three young workers from a Scottish fish farm and blasted: 'Oh! You are the people ruining the rivers and the environment.'

December 1999

Opening a new harbour at Shoreham in Sussex: 'I could not help being struck by the rather disreputable history of the harbour. For some seven hundred years the harbour could only be described as being "of no fixed abode" and after the gale of seventeen sixty-three it had no visible means of support either. I like to think that today's ceremony has finally made an honest harbour of it.'

May 1958

Opening the Motor Show at Earl's Court: 'I am not always convinced that the driver's comfort is given enough thought. Why is it, for instance, that there is always a handle or a knob just opposite one's right knee? It may be, of course, that one should check that one is the same shape and size as the man who tested the car, but that may not always be possible. As far as the owner is concerned, beauty of line wears off very rapidly when he finds that he can reach no part of the engine without standing on his head.'

1953

During a dinner held by the Society of Motor Manufacturers and Traders, when most of the guests were smoking heavily: 'I hope your products don't make as much smoke as you do!'

October 1956

To members of the Institute of Fuel, puffing cigars at a dinner: 'It makes a rather splendid picture to see members of the Institute of Fuel smoking like the proverbial chimneys.'

November 1954

Expressing concern about the world's growing population, he suggested there should be a 'tax on babies' – despite having four children himself.

1968

'I dare say there will always be a certain number of Andy Capps (a popular cartoon character depicted as lazy and unemployed) in the community, but more leisure, education, mobility and money are going to make matters worse in a few years.'

November 1963

Opening a hydroelectric scheme at the Fasnakyle power station in the Scottish Highlands: 'There were several reasons why I accepted your invitation, not least was a wish to see for myself whether there was any justification in the criticisms that the North of Scotland Hydro-Electric Board was wantonly destroying the natural beauty spots of the Highlands.

'From what I have seen this afternoon, to suggest that the power house alone destroys the beauty of Glen Affric is being as fastidious as the fairy-tale princess who could feel a pea under fifteen mattresses.'

October 1952

On the Caribbean island of Anguilla, Philip met a rabbit breeder and told him: 'Don't feed your bunnies on pawpaw fruit – it acts as a contraceptive! Then again, it might not work on rabbits.'

February 1994

On the same visit, at the Department of Agriculture, Briton Margaret Tabor told him eight-week-old rabbits were being bred in cages for food.

'Why don't you eat the wild goats instead?' asked Philip. You only need some idiot to let some rabbits escape and they will be all over the place.'

When Margaret said she had no problems yet, he replied: 'You will have, don't worry!'

1994

In Anguilla he was told of a project to protect turtle doves from man.

'Cats kill far more birds than men,' he said. 'Why don't you have a slogan: "Kill a cat and save a bird!"?'

1994

At a bee-keeping centre in Anguilla he told researchers: 'What if you get killer bees here? The first thing you'll know about it is when they swarm down the road after you.' He then spotted bee-keeper Rudolph Gomes, who had been standing for more than an hour in his protective clothing in sweltering heat.

'Are you all right in there? You see, they tell you it's safe but look at him. The key word around here seems to be hope.'

1994

As president of the Automobile Association Philip suggested that diesel vehicle exhausts should be designed to send fumes upwards.

'If it goes upward, there is a chance of it being dispersed, before it comes down and asphyxiates all the dogs and cats.'

He also said: 'I am sure diesel smoke is shortening my life!'

June 1961

Speaking as president of the World Wildlife Fund he made it clear his purpose was not to protect all animals against everything.

'We have no intention of campaigning against mousetraps or fly-papers,' he said.

November 1962

During the television screening of his film *Around the World in Forty Minutes*, which in one scene showed a crocodile he had shot in Gambia: 'It's not a very big one, but at least it's dead and it took an awful lot of killing!'

May 1957

On a tour of the London Design Centre he was shown three types of lavatory cisterns.

'This is the biggest waste of water in the country by far,' he said. You spend half a pint and flush two gallons!'

1965

On a visit to New York he spoke of the killing of rhinoceros to use their horns as an aphrodisiac in China: 'Incomprehensible! They might as well grind up chair legs!'

1962

To the annual lunch of the Automobile Association: 'It seems absolutely fantastic that we need to have a rail strike before anyone acknowledges that a traffic problem is deemed to exist.'

1955

To a dinner of the Society of Motor Manufacturers and Traders: 'I strongly advise guests to enjoy the convenience of a car while they can. It won't be long before it will be quicker to go on foot. As it is, visitors to the Motor Show are recommended to leave their cars at home!'

October 1959

'Are we going to get sliced up ducks coming across?'

The Reptile-Keeper

'Here come the bloody reptiles.'

RELATIONS WITH THE PRESS

Not surprisingly Philip has a fairly dim view of the 'fourth estate' and has complained that he has 'become a caricature'.

Whenever he comes into contact with journalists, both from newspapers and TV, he doesn't miss an opportunity to make his feelings known!

In Bangladesh the Queen and the Duke were standing in the garden of a government building to meet guests waiting in line for a cocktail party.

Ashley Walton, then royal correspondent of the *Daily Express*, was with other members of the travelling 'Rat Pack' of reporters at the end of the line. Philip, not realising he could be overheard, turned to the Queen and grimaced: 'Here come the bloody reptiles!'

1983

When he was guest of honour at the 60th birthday dinner of the Foreign Press Association in London he described journalists as 'the people's ambassadors' but then added caustically: 'I often wish the people didn't want to know quite so much.'

1948

In 1956 the British Parliamentary Press Gallery invited him as their guest of honour and asked for his views on journalists in general: 'It is very tempting,' said Philip, 'but I think I had better wait until I get a bit older. Seriously, I think that journalism, like any other great institution in this country, is capable of both the best and the worst.

'In fact, I think that our journalism very accurately reflects our natural nature, both with the lid on and with the lid off. But personally, all I can say is that there are times when I would very much like to be a newspaper owner.'

1956

The Prince hit back at a tabloid newspaper, which had criticised the royal family, saying they were: 'unemployed, condemned to stay at home and twiddle their thumbs'.

During a Birmingham factory visit he commented with a smile: 'You know what I am doing – I am twiddling my thumbs.'

1954

On a visit to the USA in 1957 the Queen and Philip were posing for photographers on the steps of the White House.

As the royal couple turned away, an American photographer, unused to royal protocol, shouted: 'Hey, just one more!'

Philip whirled round, searching for the culprit and barked: 'What do you mean, just one more!'

1957

On a newspaper strike: 'I found it a most interesting experience – breakfast seemed to take no time at all!'

1955

At a dinner for the Newspaper Press Fund charity: 'I can't very well talk about charity all the time ... in which case I'm left with the Press, and, quite frankly, I'd rather be left with a baby!'

In the same speech: 'I don't know how easy it is for a journalist to work up a charitable frame of mind.'

1955

'When, as happens from time to time, something I have said appears in "Sayings of the Week" or similar columns, I am generally left wondering whether it was put in at its face value or whether the editor has managed to read some fearfully subtle joke into something, which I fondly imagined was quite ordinary.'

1960

To a Press Association lunch he commented on an article saying he had been over-quoted and over-photographed.

'It is encouraging to know that at least I am being killed by kindness.'

1963

'The *Daily Express* is a bloody awful newspaper.'

1962

'So you're responsible for the kind of crap Channel Four produces!' Said to Channel 4 chairman Sir Michael Bishop at a film premiere.

December 1996

At a reception for Prince Charles in Buckingham Palace he spotted a group of men he did not recognise and was told they were tabloid editors.

'It doesn't show from the outside,' he conceded generously.

November 1998

At the Newspaper Society Golden Jubilee lunch:
'And which local paper do you work for?'

'I'm terribly sorry, sir, but I'm an impostor – I'm from the Peterborough column of *The Daily Telegraph.*'

'Don't worry, it's not your fault.'

March 2002

At a press reception in Windsor Castle to mark the Golden Jubilee:

'Who are you?' he demanded of Simon Kelner.

'I'm the editor-in-chief of *The Independent*, sir.'

'What are you doing here?' asked the Duke.

'You invited me.'

'Well, you didn't have to come!'

Next victim: Martin Townsend, editor of the *Sunday Express.*

'Ah, the *Sunday Express,*' said Philip. 'I was very fond of Arthur Christiansen.'

'Yes, there's been a long line of distinguished editors,' replied Townsend.

'I didn't say that!' barked Philip, walking away.

April 2002

At a state banquet in Paris he told President Chirac: 'If we had your laws the British Press could not have done so much damage to the royal family.'

May 1996

To author Gyles Brandreth: 'I am desperate if I find there are British Press on a foreign visit. I know they'll wreck the thing if they possibly can.'

May 1999

'Philip has a fairly dim view of the "Fourth Estate".'

Prince of Ales

'I know, I'll have a beer!'

FOOD FADS AND TALES OF DRINK

Philip gave up smoking on the eve of his wedding and eats and drinks frugally. Although there were some drunken escapades in the early days of his marriage, he is now a committed weight watcher and occasional drinker, preferring half a pint of bitter to a large brandy.

At a reception in Rome he was offered the finest Italian wines by Prime Minister Giuliano Amato to wash down some exquisite young goat and chestnut: 'Get me a beer. I don't care what kind it is, just get me a beer!'

October 2000

At a reception for the US Chamber of Commerce, he was presented with a hamper of southern goods by the American ambassador in London.

He opened it and demanded: 'Where's the Southern Comfort?'

February 1999

At a banquet in Germany with the Queen, a diplomat told him: 'Try the German wine, sir, it's from the most northern vineyard in the world.'

In German he replied: 'I know, I'll have a beer!'

November 2004

Making a toast to the Land Agents Society jubilee dinner: 'Thank you very much indeed for a most excellent and enormous dinner.

'I cannot help thinking that if this is your usual standard, then I suggest that land agents should eat half as much and then we should not have to produce twice as much food.'

February 1953

At the 150th anniversary dinner of the Royal Society of Medicine: 'If I don't know anything about medicine, at least I can claim to be an expert on anniversary dinners. Nearly one hundred and fifty anniversary dinners ... what a splendid thought!

'How many tons of food, how many gallons of drink, and how many hours of speeches have gone into your history? And how many cracks about "physician heal thyself" afterwards?'

'British food is something like a small child. When it's good it's very, very good; when it's bad, it's absolutely awful.'

1964

At the Royal Cornwall Show he was offered some fish from Rick Stein's seafood deli and declined, saying: 'No, I would probably end up spitting it out over everybody.'

June 2000

At the Royal Dairy Show: 'None of the beef I have eaten at this age is edible.'

At the same show: 'Don't be put off by that look on your neighbour's face when you take as much cream as you really want. It isn't disgust that is being registered, but plain envy that you had the courage to do what he has always wanted to do and never dared.'

1965

'Where's the Southern Comfort?'

The Silent Assassin

'Dead and dying pheasants ... rained down.'

NON-VERBAL GAFFES

He doesn't even have to open his mouth to put his foot in it...

Philip was once arrested for having a royal wee in the street. In 1945, two years before he married Princess Elizabeth, he was on leave as a young naval officer in Sydney, Australia.

In 1992, former Australian detective Frank Farrell recalled he had come across Philip 'urinating on the footpath' in the harbourside area called 'The Rocks'. He said: 'I asked him what his name was and he came out with a mumble of words... He was probably fined about ten bob in those days. It was only when he married the Queen a couple of years later that I realised who he was.'

August 1945

Chatting to the Sultan of Brunei's wife, Philip made a rare non-verbal gaffe when he pointed using his index finger, an insulting gesture there.

September 1998

Royal author Brian Hoey claims Philip once knocked him over! He said: 'I was walking along a corridor in Buckingham Palace when he came out of his room looking over his shoulder and talking to someone else, and knocked me over. Without noticing what had happened, he just carried on walking.'

Story told in September 2002

When some electronic gates took a long time to open after he had zapped them with a remote control, Philip rammed his Range Rover into them, denting the front of the car.

January 2004

Schoolchildren were reduced to tears when dead and dying pheasants shot by the Duke and his party rained down on their school near Sandringham.

January 2004

'A rare non-verbal gaffe!'